SELWY

CW00407654

# Divine

# Mathematics

A biblical perspective on investing
in God's kingdom

Published 2004 by CWR, Waverley Abbey House, Waverley Lane, Farnham, Surrey GU9 8EP. Previously available as a free publication, *Service in the Eighth Degree*. This new edition contains additional material.

See back of book for list of National Distributors.

Unless otherwise indicated, all Scripture references are from the Holy Bible: New International Version (NIV), copyright © 1973, 1978, 1984 by the International Bible Society.

Concept development, editing, design and production by CWR.

Printed in England by Halstan

ISBN 1-85345-289-0

# Contents

# Introduction

One of the concerns that has weighed heavily upon me in recent years is the fact that so many Christians do not understand their relationship to the money which passes through their hands or lies in their bank or investment accounts. The truth is that once we come over on to the side of Jesus Christ then we are no longer proprietors but *stewards* of all our material resources.

As a close observer of the Christian life for over 60 years, I have come across many Christians who struggle with the whole idea of stewardship. Often it is the last thing they come to terms with in their Christian life, and some resist the idea until the end of their days. Much of this resistance is due to a failure to understand God's purposes relating to finance and a fear that, if they hand over the direction of their finances to God, He will forever keep them poor.

I hope the thoughts I have expressed in this book will help you see that the more you give to God the more you will be able to give. The idea might sound odd to some but it is based on sound biblical principles.

Read on and you will see.

Selwyn Hughes
2004

# One thing
## is sure ...

**C**an it really be true, that Christians can experience the blessing of God on their lives in a way that contributes to them making larger financial investments in the kingdom of God?

My experience tells me that it is.

Take this verse for example. I consider it to be one of the most amazing verses to be found anywhere in Scripture:

> *One man gives freely, yet gains even more; another withholds unduly, but comes to poverty.*
>
> Prov. 11:24

See what it's saying: generous giving contributes to abundance and withholding to shortage and scarcity. The operative word in the text is 'freely'. There is something about generous (and wise) giving that does something not only for those who are the recipients of the giving but for the giver also. Those who hold on to what they have and refuse to be generous towards those less fortunate than themselves may not experience poverty in financial terms, but they will undoubtedly experience it in spiritual terms.

And there can be nothing worse than poverty of the soul.

Those who believe, as I do, that the Bible contains the greatest wisdom to be found anywhere on earth, and practise its principles will know the truth of the text that has just been quoted. They find that the more they give to God, the more they have to give.

# A biblical perspective

The purpose of this booklet is to lay down a biblical perspective on the subject of giving to God. If you are not already one of those who know the experience of continual replenishment in terms of giving, I would like to show you some of the steps you need to take in order to experience this great biblical principle at work in your life.

One thing is sure – no one can claim to be a true disciple of Jesus Christ unless he or she understands the biblical principles concerning money. Our Lord had a good deal to say about money when He was here on earth. In fact 16 of His 38 recorded parables touch on the issue of finances.

Scripture fairly bulges with texts that relate to money and giving. Did you know that there are about 500 verses relating to faith, and about the same number relating to prayer, but there are more than 2,000 verses relating to the subject of money and possessions?

Let's begin with this incident in the life of our Lord:

*Jesus sat down opposite the place where the offerings were put and watched the crowd putting their money into the temple treasury.*

Mark 12:41

The Gospel writer, Mark, tells us that many rich people threw in large amounts, but a poor widow came and put in two very small copper coins worth only a fraction of a penny. As Jesus watched what was going on, He turned to His disciples and said: '... this poor widow has put more into the treasury than all the others.'

That must have caused some raised eyebrows among the disciples don't you think? By what law of mathematics does a woman who throws two small copper coins into an offering box give more than those who throw in large amounts? Jesus gave this explanation:

> 'They all gave out of their wealth; but she, out
> of her poverty, put in everything – all she had
> to live on.'

Mark 12:44

Her giving was measured not so much by what she gave but by what she had left. Does this mean that God wants us to give until we have nothing left? No, but it does introduce a whole new dimension into the matter of giving. When we give we need to focus not only on what we have given but also on what we have left.

Now, not only did Jesus sit over against the treasury in Bible days; He is sitting there still. But His purpose in sitting there, I hasten to add, is not to criticise or condemn but to help us evaluate the importance of our relationship to money. It is a solemn moment when we give of our finances with Him sitting beside us.

# Divine mathematics

The text I referred to earlier: 'One man gives freely, yet gains even more; another withholds unduly, but comes to poverty' – may seem at first to violate all the rules of mathematics. How can it be that the more you give away the more you have? It seems to defy logic.

The more I have studied Scripture the more impressed I have been with the Bible's glorious illogicality as it relates to divine mathematics. Our human system of maths says two and five make seven. But there was one occasion in Scripture where two and five added up to 5,000. Jesus Christ took two fishes and five loaves and under what Frances Ridley Havergal called 'His mighty multiplying touch' the Saviour was able to feed 5,000 people. And just to add to the point – 12 baskets of fragments were gathered up after everyone had eaten their fill! A similar story can be found in the Old Testament (2 Kings 4) where God's servant, Elisha, experienced a miraculous extension of 20 small loaves of bread which were able to satisfy 100 hungry men – with some left over.

Take this also – a statement made by Jesus: 'For whoever wants to save his life will lose it, but whoever loses his life for me will find it' (Matt. 16:25). How can someone gain by losing? The most basic profit and loss account shows a loss to be a loss and a profit to be a profit. I know of no mathematical law that says a loss can become a profit. Well, the divine scheme of things is different. We lose what is of no eternal value to gain that which lives on throughout eternity.

There is an intriguing verse found in the book of Ecclesiastes – another book written by wise old Solomon – which reads thus:

> *Though one may be overpowered,*
>   *two can defend themselves.*
> *A cord of three strands is not quickly broken.*
>
> Eccl. 4:12

Dig into the context of this verse and you discover it is talking about friendship. Verse 9 says:

> *Two are better than one,*
>   *because they have a good return for their work:*
> *If one falls down,*
>   *his friend can help him up.*
> *But pity the man who falls*
>   *and has no-one to help him up!*

Then comes the verse I have already referred to: 'Though one may be overpowered, two can defend themselves. A cord of three strands is not quickly broken.'

Why is it that the writer who has been talking about one friend with another, making *two*, adds this strange climax:

'A cord of *three* strands is not quickly broken' (my italics)? This text is often separated from its context and made to mean that three people when working together form a powerful force. But that is not what it is saying.

The *NIV Study Bible* describes the statement as a 'climactic construction' – a literary device for the sake of emphasis. But it is much more even than that. What the text is saying is this: when you are in a close relationship with another person, you not only have what the other person gives you in the friendship, or you give to the other person, but a third quality appears – a strength and power which comes out of the relationship which you could never have known apart. Your strength plus your friend's strength produce a new and even greater strength.

God makes it possible for us to give and give again.

In Solomon's day, though they understood the concept, they were not able to express it in a single word. Today we call it – *synergism*. The dictionary meaning of synergism is this: 'the combined effect of two things that exceeds the sum of their individual effects.' God has designed good close relationships in such a way that one and one does not just add up to two – one and one makes *three*.

There is, as I said before, a glorious illogicality about divine mathematics. How can one little jar of flour and one small jug of oil be used to supply the needs of a widow for weeks and weeks and weeks? It doesn't make sense. It defies logic. But you can read about this story in the 17th chapter of the first book of Kings. A widow who ministered to the needs of the prophet Elijah was rewarded by a miracle which meant that her one little jar of flour and one little jug of oil saw no diminishment as she used them day after day after day. Logic says that when one little jar of flour and one little jug of oil have been used up then that is the end of the matter. But when God is at work logic and mathematics have to give way to a higher law – the law of the divine.

Nothing is more exciting than to see divine mathematics at work in the matter of giving. We give and when we think we have come to the end of our financial resources God makes it possible for us to give and give again. One writer, when talking about God's intervention in human affairs, said: 'Mathematics and logic have nothing to do with reality.' God is the Great Reality and when He is at work then don't be surprised if everything human is turned on its head.

Permit me to return for a moment to the story of the little boy who gave his loaves and fishes to Jesus. Suppose, just suppose, that the little boy had said to himself, 'This is for my use only and I don't intend to share it with anyone.' He would have missed seeing one of the greatest miracles of all time – the Feeding of the Five Thousand. And suppose also that the disciples, instead of serving out the multiplied bread and fishes to the crowd decided to pile them high in one corner and make a charge for them.

What do you think would have happened? Well of course we know the Lord would not have allowed them to do it, but if they had attempted to they would have disqualified themselves from the service of the One whose life was given over to generosity. It is likely we would have never heard of them again.

I am sure that you come across opportunities to be generous almost every day and if you fail to respond to those opportunities who knows what rivers will not flow, what great ministries will never come to birth, what mighty things will not get done? God has opened the doors of generosity to you; don't fail to open up the doors of generosity to others.

# The effect of money on the soul

Take it from someone who has had a lifetime of experience of trying to help Christians understand their relationship to their finances, money has a very powerful and profound effect upon the human soul. I have watched hundreds of Christians in my time become financially blessed and then develop an acquisitive streak that in turn makes their souls as metallic as the coins they seek.

Someone has said that 'having a good deal of money does not change a person, it merely unmasks them'. If a person is naturally selfish or greedy, money will simply show up those tendencies in a greater and clearer light. 'An offering,' said one writer, 'is minted personality.' We can tell a lot about the kind of person we are by what and how we give.

There is no surer way of determining our spiritual maturity than by the attitude we take towards money. A pastor tells how his church began a building extension programme, and one woman, an apparently devout but financially deprived soul, used to say to him whenever he paid her a pastoral visit, 'If I had lots of money believe me I would give liberally to the building programme of the church.'

It so happened that well before the building was

completed and the church was still far from reaching its budget, the woman concerned inherited a very large legacy. She revealed this fact one day to the pastor who, on one of his pastoral visits several weeks later, reminded her of how she used to say, 'If I had lots of money I would give liberally ...'. She replied, 'Do you know, it is a strange thing; when I had no money I had the heart to give. Now that I have money I just don't have the heart!'

> Money is a wonderful servant but a terrible master.

I have known many people, too, who said they wanted to go into business to make money so that they could give it to God but once they prospered they were loathe to invest it in the kingdom. Money is a wonderful servant but a terrible master. If money is your god then your enfeebled personality is the price you pay for the worship of that god.

We had better master money before it masters us.

# Seduction
## of the soul

I t is sad how the longing for money can create a fever in the soul. It is not the possession of money but the passion for it that the Bible is against. These warnings are there because God knows that no one can live in this world without money. The more some people have the more they want and not always for itself but rather for the sense of power that the possession of money gives. The luxuries of one generation become the necessities of the next, and before long money fastens its grip.

So the Bible sounds its warning. It tells us money can seduce the soul from its true anchorage in God. It must be watched, not because it can be stolen, but because it can steal. It can steal control of a person's life.

Yours and mine.

Scripture teaches us that neither asceticism nor avarice are a balanced approach to life. It shows us that we have a right and a duty to have our needs met. In the Early Church those who had much, shared with those who had little. In Acts we see how distribution was to everyone as they had need.

*There were no needy persons among them. For from time to time those who owned lands or houses sold them, brought the money from the sales and put it at the apostles' feet, and it was distributed to anyone as he had need.*

Acts 4:34

And Scripture teaches us also that when we have more than we need we have a responsibility to help those who are in need.

Consider these words of Jesus in the well-known story of the farmer who went forth to sow. He mentioned two things that choked the growing wheat and made it unfruitful – the worries of this life and the deceitfulness of wealth (Matt. 13:22). James Moffatt translates this verse:

*As for him who is sown 'among thorns', that is the man who listens to the word, but the worry of the world and the delight of being rich choke the word; so it proves unfruitful.*

Note the words *'the delight of being rich'*. Riches are not the enemy; it is the *delight* of being rich that we have to guard against. It sours the soul when we see riches as an end in themselves. If the delight is in what can be done through riches to help others then the soul is saved from decay.

There is an old saying that whoever craves wealth for its own sake is like a man who drinks sea water, the more he drinks the more his thirst increases until finally he drinks himself to death.

Is it wrong to have riches? No. God does not condemn a Christian for that. He does condemn Christians, however, when they put their trust in riches. This is how the apostle Paul puts it when writing to Timothy:

*Command those who are rich in this present world not to be arrogant nor to put their hope in wealth, which is so uncertain, but to put their hope in God, who richly provides us with everything for our enjoyment.*

1 Tim. 6:17

The psalmist said it like this:

*Do not trust in extortion*
  *or take pride in stolen goods;*
*though your riches increase,*
  *do not set your heart on them.*

Psa. 62:10

'Money amassed has gravitational force,' says Greg Lafferty, a teaching pastor in one of America's large churches. 'It's got power, it's got pull, it's got weight. And like everything that has mass, it exerts a gravitational pull.' He recommends that we would all do well to keep one of the proverbs of Solomon always at the forefront of our mind lest we be overtaken by the snare that money and possessions can bring. Listen again to what wise old King Solomon said:

*Keep falsehood and lies far from me …*
*Otherwise, I may have too much and disown you*
    *and say, 'Who is the LORD?'*

Prov. 30:8

In order to avoid the traps that money can bring it is important to follow some simple but clear biblical principles, the first of which I suggest is this:

### Transfer ownership of your possessions to God

The very first thing a Christian should understand in relation to money and possessions is about turning them over into God's hands. Dr E. Stanley Jones, one of my spiritual mentors, used to say: 'A road that perhaps more than any other leads to self-atrophy is undedicated money.' So, if you haven't done so, then consider transferring your possessions and money over to Him today. When you let go of your possessions and let God have them, then life takes on a sense of stewardship. It really does.

'I am not the owner, I am the ower.'

Perhaps a question we ought to ask ourselves before going any further is this: who owns my possessions, does God or do I? Whether we acknowledge it or not we are only in possession of our possessions for a brief period.

If in reality we don't own our possessions then the obvious thing is to acknowledge this in a prayer to God.

Have the sense to say to Him, 'I am not the owner, I am the ower.' A businessman once said, 'I've prospered in my business; now my task is to know how much I can keep for my own use.' That's the right order. How much can I keep for myself? For everything I *needlessly* spend on myself is taken from some other person's need.

# At God's disposal

S ince we belong to God then all we have belongs to God. Unless we are willing to accept this there is little point in reading on. We must see ourselves as stewards not proprietors, not only of our treasure but also of our time and our talents.

'The earth is the LORD's and the fulness thereof' said the psalmist (Psa. 24:1, RSV). If you have been acting as though you are the owner then abdicate from the throne of your heart and let God be God. The relationship is then pegged down. That is the starting point which once accepted means we can work forward.

Putting our possessions at God's disposal does something more than settle a money issue. It settles a life attitude. You are then a person under orders, a person with a sense of mission, a sense of direction and a life goal. You realise you are handling something on behalf of Another, the 'Another' being God. That does something to the whole of life – puts sacredness into the secular, lifts the sordid into the sacred. Money becomes a message.

If money is unsurrendered to God, it soon masters us. When we hold it as a trust it blesses us. Our Christianity functions in and through the material. If we are faithful with material power, then God will entrust us with spiritual power.

Another thing our Lord said about money is this:

*'No-one can serve two masters. Either he will hate the one and love the other, or he will be devoted to the one and despise the other. You cannot serve both God and Money.'*

Matt. 6:24

The fact that *Money* has a capital letter in the text is informative. In the original Greek the word was *Mammon* with a capital 'M'. It suggests that for some people Money with a capital 'M' is on the same level as God. While money with a small 'm' is neutral, money with a capital 'M' is not.

**Let God be God.**

As Greg Lafferty reminded us, 'Money like everything that has mass exerts a gravitational pull.' You can very easily get drawn into its orbit and it becomes the centre of things for you and bends your will towards it, making you its slave. Remember this: you can't serve God and Money but you can serve God with money.

Abraham provides an excellent example in Scripture of how to transfer ownership of possessions to God. He placed his son on the altar and was willing to part with him if that was what God wanted (Gen. 22). If you have never done so then picture yourself kneeling before God's altar like Abraham. Offer up to Him all your possessions in a moment of prayer. Be prepared to die emotionally to money. Tell God that from now on there will not be two masters in your life – just one.

Him!

Transferring ownership to God means that every decision as to how your money will be earned or used will be based on scriptural principles, remembering that one day we will have to give an account to God of how we managed the funds that He entrusted to us. So tell Him that from now on you are no longer a proprietor but a steward.

# Investing in
## the kingdom

**B**ecome rich towards God by giving. We come now to another principle to follow. By far the wisest and most rewarding investments we can make while we are on this earth are those that are given to God for the furtherance of His work. If you are wealthy you are under an obligation to use some of that wealth to advance the cause of Jesus Christ.

Scripture is replete with commands and promises regarding the need to lay up treasures in heaven rather than on earth. If Jesus walked into our churches today, in the same way as He did in the synagogues when He was here on earth, I think we would hear Him say this to today's consumer society:

> 'Do not store up for yourselves treasures on earth, where moth and rust destroy, and where thieves break in and steal. But store up for yourselves treasures in heaven, where moth and rust do not destroy, and where thieves do not break in and steal. For where your treasure is, there your heart will be also.'
>
> Matt. 6:19–21

This saying of Jesus is one of the most counter-cultural statements in the whole of Scripture. Our Lord is telling us first that if we are going to be right about money then we have got to have the right storehouse. 'Do not store up for yourselves treasures on earth,' He said, 'but store up for yourselves treasures in heaven.'

So it is not wrong to store up money. In fact Christ commands it. But the crux of the matter is *where* we store our money. Store it up in heaven, says Jesus, not on earth. By that He means making investments in the things that will endure in eternity.

Our Lord makes three significant points in the statement quoted above.

1. Treasure on earth is susceptible to corruption, decay and theft. Money stored in heaven is safe and secure.

2. Treasure in heaven gets a high yield. Here we may get 5%, 15% 25% or, in a huge economic boom, some investments may return as much as 30%. Scripture talks about a thirty, sixty or even a hundredfold return.

3. Treasure and our hearts interact together. Initially your treasure goes where your heart goes. If you have your heart set on a new car or a bigger house or a computer upgrade then there is little doubt that in due course your money is going to follow your heart. Your heart then becomes all the more attached to that thing. We

are going to have to lead our hearts to heaven by investing our resources there.

People often ask me if it is a scriptural principle to save. Most definitely. Look to the ants, says the book of Proverbs, who in good seasons store up for the lean times to come (Prov. 30:25). There is biblical wisdom in saving. But millions? Why sacrifice present kingdom impact for a future on earth that has no guarantee it will ever come? We must let Jesus speak with full force into our lives. We are not just being wicked if we pile up treasures on earth; we are being stupid!

So stop storing up resources on earth. If you have enough then why want more? Enough is enough. Use that money for investing in God's kingdom. One man I heard of, having read the phenomenally popular *Prayer of Jabez* by Bruce Wilkerson, added another room to his house just to show his neighbours how God was prospering him. He didn't need the extra room so in my opinion it was a shameful waste of the Lord's money.

> Money stored up in heaven is safe and secure.

Many people spend the first half of their lives expending health to gain wealth and then the last part of their lives expending wealth to gain health.

A pastor I know tells the story of how a farmer gave $5 a year to the work of the church. One day as the pastor visited the farm, the man said, 'While you are here I will write you out my annual gift to the church.' The minister said, as he watched him write out the cheque for $5, 'All that God has done for you in this farm, which is clearly prospering and you give this! You ought to give God $500 as a thank offering.' And he added, 'God gives sunlight, soil, rain and atmosphere to bring forth a crop. That's about 93 per cent of the work, leaving only 7 per cent dependent on you. I'm surprised God doesn't paralyse your arm when you write out such a miserly amount!'

**Be rich towards God.**

That's not the best way to approach someone but in this case it worked. Those blunt words struck home. The farmer dropped to his knees and surrendered both himself and his money to God. He went into the house and told his wife what had happened. She said, 'I have been praying for this for years.' His whole life was loosed. The pastor said that for years the man gave to the church not $5 a year but $5,000.

Be rich towards God. That is where the greatest riches are. You may not be a millionaire on earth but you can be a millionaire in heaven.

# Loving
## to give

**A**nother important thing Jesus said was this:

*'The eye is the lamp of the body. If your eyes are good, your whole body will be full of light. But if your eyes are bad, your whole body will be full of darkness. If then the light within you is darkness, how great is that darkness!'*

Matt. 6:22–23

Now what that means is quite simple. There's light in the place where you are reading this, either daylight or artificial light. If your eye works and takes light in, then by that light you are able to read. If your eye does not work then though there may be light all around, you are in a sense in darkness.

Our generosity will determine how much spiritual light we have within our being. If we have a greedy eye our whole being will be filled with spiritual darkness but if we have a generous eye our whole being will be filled with spiritual light. Our bodies go where our eyes are looking. The love of money is a root of all kinds of evil says Paul to

Timothy (1 Tim. 6:10). Not money, the love of it. 'Some people, eager for money [with eyes for money], have wandered from the faith and pierced themselves with many griefs.' We have got to know what's important and what's not. We have to start acting like people who are going to live for ever.

How do we keep from amassing money and getting pulled into its orbit? Don't stockpile it on earth. Send it on to heaven. Invest it in kingdom ministry and your heart will start to be pulled there. Send the rest of it ahead so there is no gravitational pull to this world. Why would you need a stack of notes in heaven? We are only here for a short time so send it on ahead because that is where we will be spending eternity.

Greed is different from other sins, that is why Jesus describes it as an eye sin. It darkens our eye spiritually. Greed hides itself. It blinds you in a way that other things do not. Hardly anyone considers themselves greedy. If you want to know whether you are or not then ask yourself how much you dislike it in others. We can't see it. It blinds us to our own condition.

David Livingstone said these immortal words:

*If anything I have will advance that kingdom it shall be given or kept, as by giving or keeping it I shall best promote the glory of Him to whom I owe all my hopes both for time and eternity.*

That should be the motto of every Christian, put up somewhere and repeated every day. I came across this some time ago and I wrote it down in my notebook of pertinent sayings: 'Some give like a rock only when they are struck. Others give like a sponge only when they are squeezed. Others give like the flowers because they love to give.' What kind of giving characterises you?

If you dislike rich people, or feel superior to them, this shows money has power over you. I live in a flat but I confess there are times when I wish I had a pool I could swim in every morning, a house with a large garden and enough money to pay a gardener to look after things. But at such times I read Psalm 73 and come back to the biblical realisation that the greatest blessing in life is to be a child of the living God.

**What kind of giving characterises you?**

Give enough money away that sacrifices your lifestyle. If there is not sacrifice in our lives there is no joy in our lives. If there is no cross in our economic life then there is no true elation. Jesus gave His all for us. Not one tenth of His life but all. There has, therefore, to be a cross in our giving. If we give away money and it doesn't cut into the way we live and make a difference in our lifestyle then it is possible we are not responding to Jesus in the way He ministers to us.

Another principle to keep in mind is this:

## Develop a worldwide vision

So many Christians lack a worldwide vision. A Christian should have a vision for the world even though he or she is not able to go to every part of it. Our trouble today is that we are far too parochial in our vision. The apostle Paul when writing to Timothy calls the Church to prayer, showing that our prayer concerns should cover more than just the people in our own community but, rather, everybody.

> *I urge, then, first of all, that requests, prayers,*
> *intercession and thanksgiving be made for everyone –*
> *for kings and all those in authority, that we may live*
> *peaceful and quiet lives in all godliness and holiness.*
> *This is good, and pleases God our Saviour …*
>
> 1 Tim. 2:1–3

The Church then is to take everybody into the embrace of its concern and prayer. Now I am afraid this immediately rebukes many of our evangelical churches whose perspective, if we are frank, is more parochial than global.

The British preacher and writer, John Stott, tells of visiting a village church while on holiday and slipping into the back, incognito. The pastor was away and one of the leaders was taking the meeting. He prayed that the pastor might have a good holiday, mentioned certain members of the church who were sick, and that was it. No prayer for the needs of the world, the tension in different countries.

John said to himself: this is a village church with a village God. There was no thinking about the oppressed, the poor, the refugees, the place of violence, world evangelisation, famines, things that ought to concern us.

Does your local church have a worldwide vision? Then fine. Get behind it. If it doesn't, then pray that it will. It is of prime importance that you support the work of your local church but be open to the needs of parachurch organisations also. There are things they can do that a local church cannot.

> A Christian should have a vision for the world.

Not all Christians will fall within the category of my next suggestion but even if you find that you are not included don't skip over it as the point being made may apply to you at some later date.

## Making money for God

There are certain people who are gifted to make money in their business for God. We read about this gift in Romans 12. Among the gifts mentioned there is the gift of giving. After I had given a Bible study on the gifts listed in Romans 12, a man asked me this question (somewhat facetiously I think): 'If I do not have the gift of giving, does that mean that I do not have to give?'

I replied, 'No, Scripture teaches that everyone is required to give, but some have a special gift that enables them to make wise investments or establish sound businesses so that they can make a special contribution to God's Church and Christian causes.'

God calls some people to go into business as definitely as He calls some into the Christian ministry. There they may use their powers of expansion for God.

Someone asked a woman who had given her life to the cause of street children what made her do it. She said, 'I looked into the faces of the street children and then I looked into the face of Christ and I gave my life to bring the two of them together.'

I can imagine a businessman or woman saying the same, 'I looked into the faces of the needy in this world and gave my life to business in order to help meet that need.' It is not enough to build a business in order to help your family and educate your children and so on – there must be a bigger vision than that. Many business people get bogged down with making money and have no concern for the rest of the world. If it is not for the world's poor then for some other area of need, some point of concern.

A businessman came to me when I was a pastor in a London city church and said he wanted to start a business and would I pray with him. Before I prayed I asked him, 'What is the purpose of your business?' He replied, 'To provide for my family, to educate my children and to leave an inheritance for my family.' I said, 'If that is your only goal I am afraid I can't pray with you … what about the needs of the world, the Church, the poor and so on?'

That led to a very interesting conversation that went on for several hours and which resulted in that man going into business with a lightness of step, a sureness of direction and a sense of mission. He committed himself to the goal of not just meeting the needs of his family but giving away as much as possible to the work of God. As he launched his business I arranged a special commissioning service for him. I told the people gathered that he had been called to ministry to use his special gifts for the expansion of the work of God.

A story is told of a visitor to London during the time of the construction of St Paul's Cathedral, the architect of which was Sir Christopher Wren. He stopped at the construction site and asked some of the workmen what they were doing. One said, 'I am working to get money to keep my family.' Another said, 'I am working here because this is the kind of work I have been trained to do.' A third man said, 'I am helping Sir Christopher Wren build a great cathedral.'

We are here on earth not simply to work and take care of our families; we are here to help Jesus Christ build His kingdom and to help carry His message to the ends of the earth. When we understand and do this then we experience a firm sense of cosmic backing. We are creators working under the great Creator.

Another key thought to remember in this matter of giving is this:

## Generosity brings joy to the soul

Ready for another text from Proverbs? Listen to this:

*A generous man will prosper;*
  *he who refreshes others will himself be refreshed.*

Prov. 11:25

Generosity is a favourite subject of Proverbs. The generous person finds that the greatest joy in giving is to be the one who gives. When we move out of ourselves and give to others, we ourselves are refreshed. And how!

A little while ago I met a childhood friend whom I had not seen for 40 years. In fact we became Christians at around the same time. I remembered him as a somewhat mean and stingy individual and when I enquired about his work he told me that he had made enough money in construction to take early retirement. 'So what do you do with your time?' I asked.

> The generous hand comes from a generous heart.

'When I retired,' he said, 'I established a Trust into which I put all the finances I possessed, keeping back a small portion for my wife and family and our daily living. The greatest joy of my life nowadays is to distribute the millions of pounds I made in business to where God directs me.' I could see by the radiance in his countenance the truth contained in the text I just quoted: 'he who refreshes others will also be refreshed.'

Now we must not take this to mean that we ought to focus on being generous because it brings us rewards. Generosity that is exercised simply for the purpose of reward is not true generosity. The refreshment that comes from giving comes as a by-product of the giving. I once heard a critic of Christianity say, 'Christians give to others not because it is the right thing to do but because it makes them feel good. It really is a sophisticated form of selfishness – giving in order to receive.' Well, there may be some who give in order to get but, as a firsthand observer of the Christian life for well over 50 years, I have found that the great majority of Christians give simply because their hearts are overflowing with a generosity that comes from an appreciation of God's largeheartedness in giving His Son to be their Saviour. His generosity generates theirs.

The generous hand comes from a generous heart. If the heart is not generous then however much the hand gives there is no true generosity. No other section of society, I believe, is as generous as the Christian community. True Christians give not simply to get a blessing, but to be a blessing.

# The faith
## promise

Let me come finally to an issue that I believe can transform your entire perspective in relation to giving and enable you to know the joy not only of giving, but giving again and again and again.

In Paul's second letter to the Corinthians chapter 8, the apostle makes one of the strongest financial appeals I have ever read, making the point that Christ who was rich for our sakes became poor, that we through His poverty might become rich (8:9).

It appears that a year earlier the Corinthians had promised to help meet the financial needs of the Christians in Macedonia and now Paul asks them to fulfil the promise they had made 'and not let those good intentions go stale' (8:11, *The Message*).

What a powerful appeal the apostle makes as his heart, burning with passion and love for the work of the Lord in the Early Church, leads him to send Titus and another colleague to bring pressure to bear upon the hearts of the Corinthians in reminding them of their solemn promise made a year ago.

With no cheques, no postal service, no banking facilities, in order that the matter now be expedited, Paul arranges for some responsible brethren to collect the amount that had been promised.

Paul reminds them this is therefore not an issue of extortion and because of the promise they had made he promises them that God would make all grace abound to them and they would have sufficient in all things (9:8). Underline that promise in your Bible.

When you give to God you are placing your life in the flow of His eternal power and His promise is that you will always have sufficient. And what more than that could a Christian want.

**His promise is that you will always have sufficient.**

Have you ever made a faith promise to God? Countless Christians, I have discovered, have never known the deep spiritual joy that comes through doing this. Many, if not most, have spent their Christian lives just dipping in their purses whenever they feel there is a need and although this method of giving has its place and is a highly commendable attitude of giving and one which rejoices the heart of God, it is a million miles from the real life of partnership which comes from proving the Lord in a faith promise.

It requires very little faith, for example, to give a cash offering to the Lord. Sacrifice perhaps, but faith – no. You have it so you give!

# Prayerful commitment

There is much to be learned and experienced and enjoyed, however, in the fulfilment of a faith promise. A faith promise is when you sit down and work out by faith just what you will give to God in the next year or six months. Once you have committed yourself carefully and prayerfully then you set in motion the law of faith. Every month you have to trust God to help you meet the challenge of your own faith and as you pursue this there comes a widening of vision, an enlargement of faith, a capacity to believe beyond human understanding and an awareness of God in personal dealings that has to be experienced before it can be believed.

People who give this way claim that this exercise flexes the muscles of faith so much that they can believe not only for the fulfilment of their faith promise but for many other things in other areas of their lives.

I was first introduced to this concept by Dr Oswald Smith, the famous missionary pastor of The People's Church, Toronto. In an article I read he told of his reaction the first time the idea of a faith promise was presented to him. He was sitting on the platform in a certain service when a steward brought him an envelope on which were printed the words:

*'In dependence upon God I will endeavour during the coming year to give the sum of …….. towards the work of missions.'*

He watched as everyone else in the service bowed their heads in prayer looking for God's guidance and he followed their action by bowing his head and asking the Lord how much he should give. He felt the Spirit whisper to him: 'Fifty dollars.' He was shocked. It was a time of great economic trial, prices were high and fifty dollars in those far-off days was a large sum. Besides he had a family to keep, a house to buy and he was only getting a very small wage from his church. He thought he had misheard so he asked the Lord again, 'How much?' He says the Spirit seemed to whisper to him: 'How much can you trust Me for, not how much do you have? Fifty dollars.'

Oswald Smith says, 'My hand trembled as I filled in my name and address and put fifty dollars on the card and in the envelope.' But he adds, 'There came to my heart such a peace and I realized that there that moment I had received the greatest blessing of my life.'

God helped him to meet that faith promise. The following year he doubled it. The next year he doubled that and so on until The People's Church, Toronto has become one of the most famous churches in the world for its consistent missionary giving.

# Bigger and
## greater things

**A** faith promise provides you with a purpose to give and a purpose to pray and stimulates your faith towards bigger and greater things and opens up the blocked channels of your life that fear and unbelief may have clogged.

Many years ago when I was a pastor in a London church, I invited every church member at the beginning of the year to make a faith promise to God. Everyone took some time to pray over the matter and then put the figure they thought God wanted them to give on the faith promise card.

Later, when recording the cards in the Church Faith Promise Register, I noticed the name of an old widow whose circumstances I was very familiar with. I was somewhat surprised at the comparatively large amount she had put on her card and later I went to see her to find out if she had made a mistake.

'This is the amount I believe the Lord will enable me to give.'

When I raised the matter that I considered her faith promise too large and that she ought to consider reducing it, she burst into tears. At first I thought they were tears of relief but eventually she turned to me and said, 'Pastor, that is the figure the Lord told me to give – are you trying to stop me proving the Lord? This is the amount I promised to give and this is the amount I believe the Lord will enable me to give.'

I felt rebuked and didn't quite know what to do. I apologised for my remarks and left the matter as it was. I watched the progress of her giving very carefully in the months that followed, and to my surprise and astonishment she fulfilled her promise on a monthly basis until every penny had been paid.

This woman had only meagre savings and where the money came from I have no idea. On one occasion a friend of hers told me that members of her family who previously had given her very little financial help, began to send her regular financial gifts.

I think of this old widow often. She has gone to be with the Lord now and just days prior to her death she withdrew her small savings and sent it to the organisation I serve – Crusade for World Revival – with a note saying: 'I don't have long in this world now – this might be the last time I can give to God in this way. Use it for His work and His service.'

As I look back I tremble to think that I came close to hindering a woman from entering a dimension of giving that the Lord had been leading her into. Her Saviour had been drawing her into a place where He would prove Himself to be no man's debtor. I'll never thank God enough for the lesson that widow showed me by her faith and confidence in God.

# Making a
# faith promise

I invite you to make a faith promise to God now. Start by asking God to help you work out the right amount – an amount beyond your tithe – that will stretch your faith a little. Do not make it too large. Your faith might be very high after reading this, but start at the lowest point of your faith. There must be no strain, no anxiety, no fear. One thing is sure – your giving will open up the flow of God's power in your life.

Some months before writing this booklet I sat down and made my faith promise for the year ahead. I asked the Lord how much I should give. The amount that came into my mind in answer to that prayer seemed astonishing. My reaction was to say, 'Lord, are you sure?' I went ahead and made my commitment. Within a few weeks of making that commitment I was offered a writing contract that gave me much more than I planned to give.

Many of my friends and colleagues tell similar stories following their commitment to the making of a faith promise. It seems God delights to enter into partnership with us in relation to giving by faith, and as we work God works. So make a start. Give God an opportunity to multiply your ability to give and increase your faith by first committing yourself to give a certain amount to Him.

The question might arise in your mind: where do I give beyond my tithe? A good guide is to look prayerfully into your heart and try to ascertain where your particular 'burden' might lie. God often burdens Christians to pray for and give to certain causes. Not everyone will have the same burden. God has given me a great burden for children who have been orphaned, abused or are in desperate circumstances and that is where most of my giving is directed.

> Your giving will open up the flow of God's power in your life.

With you it might be in other directions: evangelism and the propagation of the gospel, relief for the poor, helping Christians in the developing world to have great access to spiritual resources, and so on. Pray and ask God to show you not just how much you should give but also where you should give.

Then, when you have decided, photocopy and fill in the Faith Promise Pledge Card at the back of this book and send it to the organisation concerned. If you decide to give to CWR, the organisation I represent, then fine, but my concern in writing this booklet is not specifically to raise funds for CWR but, first, to help encourage you to develop your faith and, second, to release a flow of finance into those organisations who are involved in the affairs of His kingdom and who need financial assistance in the work that God has called them to do.

# Criteria to follow when giving

**W**hen giving to a Christian organisation ask yourself the following questions:

- Is the ministry one which honours Christ and the Word of God?

- Does it teach and maintain godly standards?

- Is there evidence of God's blessing on the work?

- Is it based on sound doctrine? (Doctrinal error will eventually destroy a ministry.)

- Do its leaders demonstrate a simple and basic lifestyle and are not given to lavish living?

- Does the organisation show evidence of careful and prudent financial management?

*And God is able to make all grace abound to you, so that in all things at all times, having all that you need, you will abound in every good work.*

2 Cor. 9:8

*Remember this: Whoever sows sparingly will also reap sparingly, and whoever sows generously will also reap generously. Each man should give what he has decided in his heart to give, not reluctantly or under compulsion, for God loves a cheerful giver. And God is able to make all grace abound to you, so that in all things at all times, having all that you need, you will abound in every good work. As it is written:*

*'He has scattered abroad his gifts to the poor;*
*   his righteousness endures for ever.'*

*Now he who supplies seed to the sower and bread for food will also supply and increase your store of seed and will enlarge the harvest of your righteousness. You will be made rich in every way so that you can be generous on every occasion, and through us your generosity will result in thanksgiving to God.*

*This service that you perform is not only supplying the needs of God's people but is also overflowing in many expressions of thanks to God. Because of the service by which you have proved yourselves, men will praise God for the obedience that accompanies your confession of the gospel of Christ, and for your generosity in sharing with them and with everyone else. And in their prayers for you their hearts will go out to you, because of the surpassing grace God has given you. Thanks be to God for his indescribable gift!*

2 Cor. 9:6–15

# The truth about tithing

There is a great difference of opinion among Christians in relation to tithing. Some say it is an Old Testament law and really does not have any place in the New Testament. I myself believe that it does have New Testament support and the practice of it is a good place to begin when talking about our financial responsibility as Christians.

Tithing was actually established prior to the law being given to Moses (see Gen. 14:20). It was reaffirmed by Christ in the New Testament (see Matt. 23:23). The tithe is the first ten per cent of our income (see Deut. 14:22–23). This belongs to the Lord. There are some Christians who think that once they have tithed, their responsibility towards God has ceased. They use the tithe as a mental licence to do what they like with the nine-tenths that is left. To buy off God, so to speak. That is not what stewardship is all about. We are to use the nine-tenths wisely also and under God's direction for, as we have seen, everything we have belongs to the Lord.

The tithe serves the practical function of supporting the vital ministries of the local church – ministries such as reaching non-Christians with the gospel, ministering to the sick, caring for the widows, distributing to the needs of the saints, giving to the poor and, of course, supporting those who are involved in the full-time ministry of the Church. If a local church is not engaged in these ministries then it is doubtful that it has a right to call itself a Christian church. In such a situation some serious discussion needs to take place with those responsible for the running of the church. The tithe is in danger of being misused.

The Bible also encourages us to give offerings above and beyond the tithe. In a sense it is true to say that one cannot give an offering until the tithe has been paid. And we ought to see the tithe also as applying to more than money. Our Lord, as you will see from the statement that follows, commended those who tithed part of their harvest, but He also warned them not to neglect such important issues as justice and the love of God.

**The Bible also encourages us to give offerings above and beyond the tithe.**

*'Woe to you Pharisees, because you give God a tenth of your mint, rue and all other kinds of garden herbs, but you neglect justice and the love of God. You should have practised the latter without leaving the former undone.'*
Luke 11:42

Scripture talks a good deal about giving the firstfruits to God.

*'Honour the LORD with your wealth, with the firstfruits of all your crops; then your barns will be filled to overflowing, and your vats will brim over with new wine.'*

Prov. 3:9–10

The ancient Israelites waved the firstfruits of the harvest before the Lord as an acknowledgment that the coming harvest belonged to Him and that they would use it accordingly. Dedicated Christians should think not only of giving the firstfruits of their finances, but also of their time. Every Christian ought to ask themselves this question: how much unpaid service do I undertake for the cause of Jesus Christ every week? And what about the first part of the day? Do we put a fence around the dawning of each new day in order to spend time with God and deepen our relationship with Him? That, to my way of thinking, is also part of the 'firstfruits'.

All this might sound very legalistic to some but there is good reason why the Lord talks to us like this in His Word, not the least being this:

*'Be sure to set aside a tenth of all that your fields produce each year … your grain, new wine and oil … so that you may learn to revere the LORD your God always.'*

Deut. 14:22–23

Note the words – *'that you may learn to revere the LORD'*. The underlying purpose of the tithe, then, is not just to provide the necessary finance for God's work, but, above all, that we may develop a reverence for Him. There is something about paying one's tithe to God that brings the soul into a sense of alertness and responsibility towards the Almighty.

Believe me, there is no greater spiritual advantage than to carry in one's heart a sense of reverence for God. Some translations, when describing the reverence we ought to have towards Him, use the phrase: 'the fear of the Lord'. There are unhealthy fears and there are healthy fears. To have in our hearts a 'fear of the Lord' does not mean that we are afraid of Him in the general sense of the word, but that we stand in awe of Him, that we respect Him and seek to live according to His Word.

Remember, what happens to your money happens to you. Your money is an extended or contracted you. If you pile up money with no purpose behind it you clutter up yourself and it becomes a purposeless self, hence an unhappy self.

# Freedom
## or legalism?

**H**ow should we pay our tithe? Scripture says 'on the first day of the week'. Here are Paul's instructions given to the Corinthian converts:

*On the first day of every week, each one of you should set aside a sum of money in keeping with his income, saving it up, so that when I come no collections will have to be made.*

1 Cor. 16:2

Permit me to tell you of a Christian businessman who told me how his reverence for God increased as he decided to pay his tithe on a weekly basis.

*At one time, I used to pay my tithe to my local church by cheque every six months. Then one day I read 1 Corinthians 16:2 where Paul talks about laying aside a sum of money in keeping with my income on the first day of the week. I decided to follow his advice and so arranged for my tithe to be put into the offering in my local church in cash every Sunday. Immediately I did this I noticed that my whole spiritual perspective changed. There was something about giving my tithe on a weekly basis that brought a new sense of personal*

*responsibility, a new awareness of my dependency on the Lord for health and guidance.*
*It transformed my giving and gave me a reverence for the Lord that was far greater than anything I ever experienced before.*

In establishing the tithe as a weekly reminder of His responsibility to God something wonderful took place in this man's soul.

'Freedom is not the right to do what we want but the power to do what we ought.'

Let me take up this point of legalism once again. There are some Christians who say that the New Testament teaches freedom and that the idea of paying a tithe on a regular and systematic basis goes against that freedom.

There is a great deal of muddled thinking in today's Church about this issue of legalism. I like what Mark Buchanan in his book *Your God is Too Safe* says on this subject:

*We are overly prone to see legalism lurking behind every exhortation to strive and make an effort to be holy. Every time I say 'work out your salvation' someone will hear me say 'work for your salvation'. The two are utterly different things.*

Something similar happens whenever the word 'tithe' is mentioned. People relate tithing to the Old Testament and cry 'legalism'. But it is not a return to the keeping of laws, rather an engaging with a truth that is laid down everywhere in the Word of God.

Regrettably, the concept of spiritual freedom is often misunderstood. We are free not to do as we like but as is required of us by God. One preacher I know defines it this way: 'Freedom is not the right to do what we want but the power to do what we ought.'

The apostle Paul put it like this:

*It is to freedom that you have been called, my brothers. Only be careful that freedom does not become mere opportunity for your lower nature.*

Gal. 5:13, Phillips

We need to be sure, when arguing against tithing, that we are not doing so because the idea of systematic giving runs contrary to our carnal nature. It is so easy to believe what we want to believe.

Scripture reminds us that we can approach God's Word from one of two directions – with a natural mind or a spiritual mind. The New King James version puts it like this:

*But the natural man does not receive the things of the Spirit of God ... nor can he know them, because they are spiritually discerned.*

1 Cor. 2:14–15

The difference between a natural mind and a spiritual mind is this: a person with a 'natural' mind uses human reasoning before deciding to obey God's Word. A person with a 'spiritual' mind begins by obeying a scriptural command and then afterwards understands the hidden wisdom and purpose behind the command.

There is great wisdom in the Scriptures which is higher than anything our minds can achieve on their own. We would do well to trust Scripture and obey its commands even though it may run counter to our natural feelings.

Consider this also: one of the most sobering truths in the Bible is that when God's people withhold their tithes they are guilty of robbing God. This is what the Lord said to His people, through His prophet Malachi:

*'Will a man rob God? Yet you rob me. But you ask, "How do we rob you?" In tithes and offerings.'*

Mal. 3:8

God goes on to say that the whole nation was under a curse because they robbed Him of their tithes and offerings (Mal. 3:9). The Almighty then reasons with them that if they brought their tithes into the storehouse He would bless them abundantly and He promises to 'rebuke the devourer' for their sakes (Mal. 3:11, NKJ).

I am absolutely convinced, through a lifetime of counselling and pastoral affairs, that many Christians suffer unnecessary financial loss because they fail to tithe.

Scripture clearly establishes a cause and effect sequence between God's commands and losing money. How much does it mean to you to know that having put God first He is there to 'rebuke the devourer' for your sake?

If we fail to apply God's principles of finance He allows riches with sorrow or the devouring of our assets. God, speaking through the prophet Haggai, makes it abundantly clear.

> We are to give Him the 'firstfruit' of all our increase.

> *"You expected much, but see, it turned out to be little. What you brought home, I blew away. Why?" declares the LORD Almighty. "Because of my house, which remains a ruin, while each of you is busy with his own house."*
>
> Hag. 1:9

Just before we leave the subject of the tithe – many people ask the question: should I tithe on my gross income or the net? Let me answer it this way: A builder who puts up a house for, say, £100,000 and sells it for £120,000 would only be expected to tithe on the net gain of £20,000. This is consistent with the command, 'Honour the LORD with your wealth, with the firstfruits of all your crops' (Prov. 3:9). On the other hand the 'net increase' is determined before taxes, social security and other deductions, since we are to give Him the 'firstfruit' of all our increase.

Consider now some practical insights into this important issue of how we handle our money.

# Responsibilities
## in the family

I said earlier that there are some Christians who think that once they have tithed their income their responsibility towards God has ceased and they are then free to do as they like with the other nine-tenths. That is not what stewardship is all about. The giving of the tithe is an acknowledgment that the nine-tenths also belongs to God. We are therefore to use it wisely and under God's direction for, as we have seen, everything we have belongs to the Lord.

Let's consider a few guidelines that relate to how we ought to handle the money in our possession after we have paid our tithe. As I said earlier I am not a financial expert but what I am going to say now is based on a biblical perspective of finances and my experience in dealing with thousands of Christians over the years on the subject of money management based on scriptural principles. I have talked these issues over with financial experts committed to a high view of Scripture and they agree in essence with what you are about to read.

First on the list are the needs of the family and the establishing of the home. God has designed the man to be the leader in the home (Eph. 5:23) and thus every man ought to make the welfare of wife and children his first priority. Fathers and mothers should be part of their joint concern also, especially if elderly.

Men are also commanded by the Lord to love their wives as Christ loved the Church (Eph. 5:25). Someone said that the best thing a man can do for his children is to love his wife – in that way the children grow up in a safe and secure atmosphere.

> The best thing a man can do for his children is to love his wife.

Married men need to understand that when God designed the husband and wife to come together in one flesh, His purpose was for the wife to provide valuable assistance in the basic areas of the husband's life. In Genesis 2:18 we read: 'The LORD God said, "It is not good for the man to be alone. I will make a *helper* suitable for him."' (my italics). God has put an instinct in a woman that in marriage can be a great help to a man when he is seeking direction and guidance in his management of the home and financial affairs.

There are several scriptural examples of God giving information to a wife before her husband. He told Manoah's wife that she would have a son and how she was to rear him, before He told Manoah (see Judg. 13:1–15). He appeared to Mary before He explained Christ's birth to Joseph (see Matt. 1:18–20). The wife of a prosperous landowner in Shunem accurately discerned the godly character of Elisha and urged her husband to assist him (see 2 Kings 4:8–9). The wife of a governing ruler in

Jerusalem discerned the innocent character of Jesus and warned her husband not to deliver Him over to judgment (see Matt. 27:19).

These scriptural examples serve to illustrate the significant ability of a wife to arrive at conclusions instinctively and a man would be wise to take advantage of this instinct that God appears to have put in women. This does not mean that a woman is always right. In Scripture there are examples, too, of women misleading their husbands. Adam and Eve are prime examples. Abraham's wife Sarah's advice that he should have a child with Hagar is another (Gen. 16:5).

The physical, spiritual and psychological needs of children must also be paramount. Scripture says that children are a gift from God (Psa. 127) and require not just food and clothing but spiritual nurturing as well.

Someone has defined childhood in this way: 'Childhood is that period of life when a mother and father build the rooms of the temple in which later God will dwell when the child becomes an adult.'

The very first objective in relation to children is character training. From birth to six years, children should be taught godly character qualities and particularly how to stand alone against evil, no matter what the cost. They should learn such things as forgiveness, accountability, a clear conscience and so on. It is essential for parents to instil in their children a basic understanding of finances as well as teaching them basic life skills.

# The lure of advertising

A nother thing parents need to do in a family is develop sales resistance to the powerful influence of alluring advertising. Alluring advertising has been defined as 'the carefully planned appeals to our human weaknesses designed to make us discontent with what we have so that we can rationalise buying things that we know we do not need and should not have'.

Impulse buying is the sure way to financial bondage. The marketplace, and the road to it, are carefully designed to trap the undisciplined shopper, but God wants us to have the discernment which Eve failed to exercise in the Garden of Eden.

Consider, for example, some of the subtle tactics of advertising such as tobacco advertisements that carry the warning 'Cigarette smoking is dangerous to your health'. Though this caution came from government and health agencies the tobacco companies are happy to include it because they know that *most people tend to believe that what happens to others will not happen to them*. They blatantly exploit that propensity in human nature to their own advantage.

Then there are those who use beautiful and successful-appearing models, communicating the message that if you buy their product you will also become attractive and successful. And what about advertisements that shout: 'Why not change your life for the better?' Such slogans create discontent by getting us to focus on what we do not have and thus they encourage instant gratification.

'Instant gratification,' said Dr Robert Schuller, pastor of the Crystal Cathedral in California, 'is responsible for many a life being shipwrecked and is the greatest hindrance to the development of character I know.'

Many advertisements also set out to make people feel guilty or appeal to pride or sloth. Be on the alert as they can inveigle money out of your pocket that ought to be put to better use. Analyse all advertising and ask for documentation for advertising claims.

Another thing a family should do to ensure financial responsibility is to regularly cast an eye over expenses with a view to reducing housekeeping bills. Learn how to get better deals and the best buys on such things as heating, lighting and telephone costs. We live in a very competitive society and Christians should be alert to how to save money as well as make it. Money saved, goes the old saying, is money earned. Thousands of pounds are being lost to the kingdom because they are being wasted in unnecessary home expenditures.

There are two ways to be wealthy, said someone. One is in the abundance of your possessions, and the other the fewness of your wants. A missionary tells of a young man who joined the missionary team in a foreign land and appeared concerned because there was a lack of the usual conveniences he was used to. The older missionary, sensing his discomfiture, said, 'Make a list of all the things you are used to and I will show you how to do without them.' Discontent destroys our ability to enjoy the things God has given us since our focus is on the things we think that He should give us rather than on what we do have.

Contentment with basics equips us to resist the continuous barrage of advertising seeking to convince us that we are not able to enjoy life unless we buy some new gadget or service. Someone has said that contented people feel wealthy because they know that they already possess more than they need for daily living. 'Godliness with contentment,' said Paul to his young assistant Timothy, 'is great gain' (1 Tim. 6:6).

> Contentment with basics equips us to resist the continuous barrage of advertising.

A billionaire, who is also a Christian, says that one of the biggest mistakes people make is to work out savings by pennies rather than percentages. He explains why it is important, for example, to save two cents on a can of soup. 'If one can costs a dollar and another of equal quality costs 98 cents you should buy the 98 cent can,' he says. Why would a millionaire talk about saving two cents? This is his reason: 'You are not just saving two cents, you are saving a percentage which if followed might possibly reduce your food bill by a great amount.' This kind of thinking perhaps shows why this man is a millionaire. His counsel is confirmed by the teaching of Christ: 'Whoever can be trusted with very little can also be trusted with much …' (Luke 16:10).

# Insurance and inheritance

Christians also should understand the principle of insurance. Some believe that insurance reflects a lack of trust in God, but the concept behind it is sharing a loss. This is a sound scriptural principle:

*Carry each other's burdens, and in this way you will fulfil the law of Christ.*

Gal. 6:2

Just be sure, however, that you do not overinsure or use insurance as a savings policy. As long as inflation is a reality of life, whole life policies that promise end-of-life dividends may be a very poor way of saving. In most cases it is wiser to buy life assurance and put the difference into other investments.

One final point in relation to the home – prepare an instructive will for your family. The potential of a will goes far beyond the disposal of property. To be done correctly a will requires much thought, prayer and preparation. A will can be a carefully compiled document drawn from what God has taught you over the years and what you want your family to learn for years to come.

God gave us two 'wills', so to speak, when He gave us the Old and New Testaments. They contain history, chronology, practical instructions and future direction. Basically, a will is a document which contains directives for the transfer of property or finance to your inheritors, but as a counsellor and a pastor I have sat with many Christians who in preparing their wills asked for my help in forming a document that would pass on to their family some of the salient lessons God had taught them in their walk with Him.

'He has helped me invest money in the right way.'

I shall never forget being present at the reading of such a will when the lawyer read out words that to the best of my memory went something like this:

*I would like my family to know that what I leave to them has been carefully evaluated and thought through in the presence of God. One of the reasons why I have been able to organise my financial affairs is because I faithfully tithed and put God first in everything. He has helped me invest money in the right way, first in His kingdom and then in other wise investments. It is because of His faithfulness and blessing that I have been able to pass on to you, the members of my family, these financial blessings. I hope that every one of you will come to know Christ in the*

*way I knew Him and now through death know him*
*better. 'O let me commend my Saviour unto you.'*
  [This final sentence was borrowed from the famous
                                words of John Wesley.]

There was not a dry eye in the room as the lawyer and
executor of the man's will read out those words and I
know for a fact that one of the grandchildren became a
Christian as a direct result of that statement.

It is important to update a will when appropriate for the
reasons which a friend of mine gave in this letter to me
following something I had written in my Bible devotional
notes, *Every Day with Jesus*.

*I write to tell you that I have made some alterations to*
*my will based on something I read in the current*
*edition of* Every Day with Jesus. *You wrote: 'You have*
*no right to leave to relatives what they do not need and*
*what God has entrusted to you to invest in kingdom*
*purposes.' In my earlier will I left everything to my*
*children so that they could finish their education, buy*
*homes for themselves and so on, but now they have all*
*carved out wonderful careers for themselves and all*
*have a solid financial foundation beneath them. Their*
*financial needs now are not the same as they were*
*twenty years ago. I considered what you wrote and*
*have now arranged for them to receive substantial*
*sums but nowhere near what they would have had if*

*my will had not been changed. Your advice on
updating one's will to take in existing circumstances is
something that every Christian ought to consider.
Please continue to emphasise this point from time to
time in your writings.*

Every Christian who has anything to leave behind in the
way of money or possessions should make a will. This
simple instrument ensures that your possessions and
money go where you want them to go and prevents your
money from going into probate court. Once you have
composed the basic content, any lawyer is able to adapt it
to legal terms and make sure it contains the necessary
items. One of the unexpected benefits of preparing a
detailed will is that potential family disagreements can be
anticipated and worked out ahead of time.

Isaac's heritage included a much-coveted verbal blessing
which he passed on to his sons (Gen. 27). Jacob's 'will'
included a detailed description of what God would do in
each of his son's lives, based on their actions, character
and abilities (Gen. 49). Recab's last will and testament
contained guidelines for self-control in living. And God
rewarded His descendents for obeying them (Jer. 35).

An old saying says, 'That which I spent I had, that which
I kept I lost, that which I gave I have.'

# Service in the
##     eighth degree

**M**any years ago a Jewish rabbi by the name of Moses Mimolidees listed eight degrees of giving.

1. Giving grudgingly
2. Giving willingly but less than one should
3. Giving only when asked
4. Giving what one should give without being asked
5. Giving when the recipients know who gave but the giver doesn't know who receives
6. Giving when the giver knows who the recipients are but the recipients don't know who the giver is
7. Giving when neither the giver nor the recipient know each other
8. When the giver helps the receiver to give to others.

This last he called 'service in the eighth degree'. It is wonderful to be a receiver but the greatest joy is to be a giver. I shall never forget a man giving to me many years ago when

I was in financial difficulties. I needed help and a businessman said to me, 'The Lord has told me to give to you but before I do I want to show you how to give to others.'

> It is wonderful to be a receiver but the greatest joy is to be a giver.

It revolutionised my life and I can honestly say that in my personal finances I have never had an occasion when I have not been able to give what I pledged. What he did for me I have done to others to whom I have been able to give.

This is how Jesus put it: *It is more blessed to give than to receive.* One of the passions of my life is to turn getters into givers. We are saved to serve, to be useful, and nothing is more powerful than giving to God. The novelist John Grisham said, 'My wife and I measure the success of each year by how much we've been able to give away.'

I give John Wesley the penultimate word: 'make all you can, save all you can, and give all you can'. But, as I am sure you will agree, Scripture must have the *last* word:

> *'Give, and it will be given to you. A good measure, pressed down, shaken together and running over, will be poured into your lap. For with the measure you use, it will be measured to you.'*

Luke 6:38

Are you a UK tax payer? UK charities are entitled to a 28% tax reclaim from the Inland Revenue on every £1 donated by UK taxpayers, therefore increasing your original gift without it costing you anything more.

You are a UK taxpayer if:
- Tax is taken from your wages or salary before you receive your pay.
- You have to fill in a self-assessment form each year.
- You have any taxable savings (in a Building Society, for instance), or a pension plan, or investment income.
- If you have recently paid any capital gains tax, or expect to pay it in the near future. This could be on the sale of a property or some shares, for example.

## And even more again for some

Higher rate taxpayers in the UK can also claim higher rate relief from the Inland Revenue on their gifts – so your contributions will personally cost you even less. Any tax you pay currently will be reduced by the difference between the higher rate (currently 40%) and the basic rate (currently 22%). Therefore giving you 18% of your original gift to give away again.

Of course not all giving needs to go to an organisation or to a charity but if you are giving to a UK registered charity (this includes most churches) this is a simple way of increasing your gift. If the organisation is not a registered charity (and therefore not subject to the charity commission checks and independent scrutiny) you may like to ask why not.

Just ask the charity that you are interested in for a Gift Aid form.

*giftaid it*

## THE FAITH PROMISE PLEDGE CARD

In dependence upon God I will endeavour during the next six months/year (cross out whichever does not apply) to give the sum of £_____ towards the work of (indicate the organisation here)

_____

I will pay this sum: monthly, quarterly, biannually, annually.

My first contribution is enclosed for the sum of

£_____

I understand that this faith promise does not commit me in any way to the payment of the full sum and that this will be forthcoming only as God helps me.

My Name_____

My Address_____

_____

_____

My Telephone No._____

My position in church, business, etc._____

_____

*One man gives freely, yet gains even more; another withholds unduly, but comes to poverty.*

Proverbs 11:24

☐ Please send me a Gift Aid form

(Send now to the charity or organisation of your choice )

This is a template for you to use or photocopy to send your gift to CWR or the charity of your choice. It has been produced by CWR in the interests of the kingdom of God.

# National Distributors

**UK: (and countries not listed below)**
CWR, Waverley Abbey House, Waverley Lane, Farnham,
Surrey GU9 8EP.
Tel: (01252) 784700  Outside UK +44 1252 784700

**AUSTRALIA:** CMC Australasia, PO Box 519, Belmont, Victoria 3216.
Tel: (03) 5241 3288

**CANADA:** Cook Communications Ministries, PO Box 98, 55 Woodslee
Avenue, Paris, Ontario.
Tel: 1800 263 2664

**GHANA:** Challenge Enterprises of Ghana, PO Box 5723, Accra.
Tel: (021) 222437/223249  Fax: (021) 226227

**HONG KONG:** Cross Communications Ltd, 1/F, 562A Nathan Road,
Kowloon.
Tel: 2780 1188  Fax: 2770 6229

**INDIA:** Crystal Communications, 10-3-18/4/1, East Marredpalli,
Secunderabad – 500026. Andhra Pradesh, Tel/Fax: (040) 27737145

**KENYA:** Keswick Books and Gifts Ltd, PO Box 10242, Nairobi.
Tel: (02) 331692/226047  Fax: (02) 728557

**MALAYSIA:** Salvation Book Centre (M) Sdn Bhd, 23 Jalan SS 2/64,
47300 Petaling Jaya, Selangor.
Tel: (03) 78766411/78766797  Fax: (03) 78757066/78756360

**NEW ZEALAND:** CMC Australasia, PO Box 36015, Lower Hutt.
Tel: 0800 449 408  Fax: 0800 449 049

**NIGERIA:** FBFM, Helen Baugh House, 96 St Finbarr's College Road,
Akoka, Lagos.
Tel: (01) 7747429/4700218/825775/827264

**PHILIPPINES:** OMF Literature Inc, 776 Boni Avenue,
Mandaluyong City.
Tel: (02) 531 2183  Fax: (02) 531 1960

**REPUBLIC OF IRELAND:** Scripture Union, 40 Talbot Street, Dublin 1.
Tel: (01) 8363764

**SINGAPORE:** Armour Publishing Pte Ltd, Block 203A
Henderson Road,
11–06 Henderson Industrial Park, Singapore 159546.
Tel: 6 276 9976  Fax: 6 276 7564

**SOUTH AFRICA:** Struik Christian Books, 80 MacKenzie Street, PO Box
1144, Cape Town 8000.
Tel: (021) 462 4360  Fax: (021) 461 3612

**SRI LANKA:** Christombu Books, 27 Hospital Street, Colombo 1.
Tel: (01) 433142/328909

**TANZANIA:** CLC Christian Book Centre, PO Box 1384, Mkwepu
Street, Dar es Salaam.
Tel/Fax (022) 2119439

**ZIMBABWE:** Word of Life Books, Shop 4, Memorial Building, 35 S
Machel Avenue, Harare.
Tel: (04) 781305  Fax: (04) 774739

**For email addresses, visit the CWR website:
www.cwr.org.uk**

**CWR is a registered charity – number 294387**

Day and Residential Courses
Counselling Training
Leadership Development
Biblical Study Courses
Regional Seminars
Ministry to Women
Daily Devotionals
Books and Videos
Conference Centre

# Trusted all Over the World

CWR HAS GAINED A WORLDWIDE reputation as a centre of excellence for Bible-based training and resources. From our headquarters at Waverley Abbey House, Farnham, England, we have been serving God's people for 40 years with a vision to help apply God's Word to everyday life and relationships. The daily devotional *Every Day with Jesus* is read by over three-quarters of a million people in more than 150 countries, and our unique courses in biblical studies and pastoral care are respected all over the world. Waverley Abbey House provides a conference centre in a tranquil setting.

**For free brochures** on our seminars and courses, conference facilities, or a catalogue of CWR resources, please contact us at the following address.
CWR, Waverley Abbey House, Waverley Lane, Farnham, Surrey GU9 8EP, UK

Telephone: +44 (0)1252 784700
Email: mail@cwr.org.uk
Website: www.cwr.org.uk

CWR CRUSADE FOR WORLD REVIVAL
*Applying God's Word to everyday life and relationships*

# Christ Empowered Living
## Selwyn Hughes

*Christ Empowered Living* is Selwyn Hughes' dynamic
core teaching in one easy to digest volume.

It will transform your life with essential principles of
Christian living and help develop your full spiritual
potential. Discover biblical insights that will
revolutionise your approach to the way you live and
help to renew your mind.

This new edition improves readability and gives larger
margins for notes.

**£7.99** (plus p&p)
ISBN: 1-85345-201-7

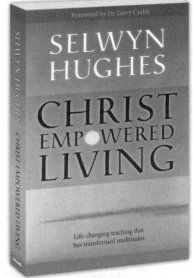

# The 7 Laws of Spiritual Success
## Selwyn Hughes

Just as there are laws in nature that hold our physical
world together, so there are laws for life that make our
spiritual walk a success. This book is Selwyn Hughes'
legacy to future generations and essential reading for
anyone who has been inspired by his teaching and ability
to apply God's Word to everyday life and relationships.

**£7.99** (plus p&p)
ISBN: 1-85345-237-8

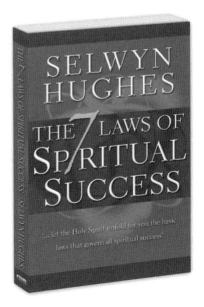